the birth date book

This Book Belongs to

The Birth Date Book

December 29

What Your Birth Date Reveals about You

Elizabeth Frankenberger

Illustrated by Claude Martinot

Ariel Books

Andrews McMeel
Publishing

Kansas City

www.andrewsmcmeel.com

ISBN: 0-8362-6390-1

Series editor: Sue Carnahan
Series design by Junie Lee
Typesetting by Ellen M. Carnahan

CONTENTS

introduction

Your birth date is more than just a passing squiggle on the calendar, more than an excuse to exceed your daily calorie ration. Your birth date is a *fateful* day; a day where the forces of the universe came together in a unique way to chart your destiny; a moment in time imprinted on your very being. Who you are, where you've been, where you're headed—all of these things had their beginning on the month, day, and hour of your birth.

The Birth Date Book sheds some light

on these influences and offers a series of snapshots of who you are. Are you glamorous and outgoing like Cindy Crawford, coolly buttoned-down like Sidney Poitier, or an unpredictable mixture of the two? Why do you prefer a particular color, taste, or scent? What career paths appeal to you? Do you harbor a secret vocation in esoteric anthropology, or does crunching numbers send you into paroxysms of joy? What about your home? Is it styled with the spacious calm of a

Zen monastery or riotously festooned like a Jamaican nightclub? Who can inspire you to drop everything and go to the ends of the earth? And who sends you running lickety-split for the nearest exit?

You'll find both surprising *and* familiar answers to these questions in the following pages. Consider this book a toast to your special day—and to the exceptional being that you are now, and continue to become every day of your life.

your astrological

Sun Sign

CAPRICORN

The key phrase for Capricorn is "I use." No two words could be more accurate! Just as the goat (the symbol for Capricorn) is notoriously able to *use* almost anything as a source of nourishment, the person born under this down-to-earth sign will usually find a way to build a modest empire from what others view as precious little. Your secret is hard work, a well-developed ability to organize, and a charmingly stubborn nature that just won't consider failure a possibility.

Capricorns are usually described as cautious, conservative, and patient. Your reserved personality quietly collects information and wisdom, molding you into a forceful, powerful, and efficient individual. Though sometimes timid, you are not afraid to provoke controversy if necessary, and you're well known for standing your ground and remaining loyal to friends and colleagues.

An out-of-balance Capricorn falls into one of two traps: You either become domineering and somewhat unforgiving, or you become unnecessarily critical, both of yourself and others. When this happens you need to fall back on your sensual, earthy nature and relax! A word of warning: The end doesn't always justify the means. Short cuts might be taken by those born under other signs of the zodiac, but for Capricorns, slow and steady is the sure route to success.

your personal
tarot card

THE WHEEL OF FORTUNE

The Wheel of Fortune is the tenth card of the Major Arcana, the twenty-two most powerful cards in the tarot deck. The Wheel is the circle of destiny, in which life and death, joy and sorrow, are tightly intertwined. For you, this means not merely taking life's ups and downs in stride, but enjoying them for the roller-coaster ride they are!

your chinese astrological symbol

Your sign comes around only once every twelve years in the Chinese zodiac, but during that year your number will definitely come up a winner in the cosmic lottery. Each sign is governed by the qualities of a particular animal guardian. Are you patient as an ox? Wise as a snake? Vain as a monkey? Locate the year of your birth in the chart below to find out—if you dare.

THE YEAR OF THE RAT

1900, 1912, 1924, 1936,
1948, 1960, 1972, 1984, 1996

Popular, ambitious, honest, and stubborn

THE YEAR OF THE OX

1901, 1913, 1925, 1937,
1949, 1961, 1973, 1985,
1997

Patient, strong, original, and rigid

THE YEAR OF THE TIGER

1902, 1914, 1926, 1938,
1950, 1962, 1974, 1986, 1998

Generous, noble, passionate, and hotheaded

THE YEAR OF THE RABBIT

1903, 1915, 1927, 1939,
1951, 1963, 1975, 1987,
1999

Discreet, sensitive, clever, and devious

THE YEAR OF THE DRAGON

1904, 1916, 1928, 1940, 1952, 1964, 1976, 1988, 2000
Enthusiastic, intuitive, shrewd, and demanding

THE YEAR OF THE SNAKE

1905, 1917, 1929, 1941, 1953, 1965, 1977, 1989, 2001
Wise, compassionate, elegant, and extravagant

THE YEAR OF THE HORSE

1906, 1918, 1930, 1942,
1954, 1966, 1978, 1990, 2002

Independent, hardworking, charming, and rebellious

THE YEAR OF THE GOAT

1907, 1919, 1931, 1943,
1955, 1967, 1979, 1991, 2003

Creative, tasteful, lovable, and fickle

THE YEAR OF THE MONKEY

1908, 1920, 1932, 1944, 1956, 1968, 1980, 1992, 2004

Witty, nimble, passionate, and vain

THE YEAR OF THE ROOSTER

1909, 1921, 1933, 1945, 1957, 1969, 1981, 1993, 2005

Frank, talented, industrious, and pompous

THE YEAR OF THE DOG

1910, 1922, 1934, 1946, 1958, 1970, 1982, 1994, 2006

Loyal, modest, intelligent, and pessimistic

THE YEAR OF THE PIG

1911, 1923, 1935, 1947, 1959, 1971, 1983, 1995, 2007

Honest, sociable, cultured, and gullible

crowning jewel

TURQUOISE

For centuries, turquoise graced the fine arts and crafts of the Native Americans. Its color, both brilliant and breathtaking, was whispered about, and the stones were lovingly carved into mystical images. Today, this stone brings you not only formidable beauty but also contentment, extraordinary luck, and even material wealth. A life of inner and outer luxury awaits!

lucky number

TEN

Ten signifies completion. It implies a hard worker who can handle life's ups and downs with equal grace. You stick to a project, finish it, then look around for the next challenge, and you generally need a sense of achievement to feel truly alive. But you are also a thrill seeker and thrive in a risky environment . . . provided that *you* are the one making the important decisions!

alphabet soup

D, L, and P

December 29s often find that names and places beginning with the following letters become especially significant during the course of their lives: *D, L,* and *P.* Your *dedication, loyalty,* and *peacefulness* will lead to a life of domestic bliss. Home becomes your castle, which you rule with a loving kindness, revealing a deep appreciation of both yourself and others.

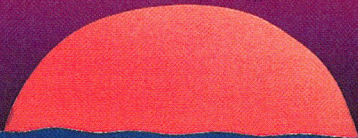

week link

FRIDAY

Friday is mystically associated with Venus, the planet of love, romance, and personal growth. This lucky connection brings both passion and harmony into your life. Luxuriate in your intriguing Venusian pastimes—a playful flirtation or an artistic project that starts your creativity flowing. Friday is the day to revel in your passions and enjoy your true nature!

your magical food

PUMPKINS

From prize-winning mega-pumpkins to palm-sized novelties, pumpkins can fill any niche. December 29s are just as versatile. You can be anything to anybody—*if* you want to. But you're unpredictable. Like a two-sided jack-o'-lantern, you might show your grinning countenance one night and your forbidding scowl the next. You're great company—but maybe not for the faint of heart!

your color cue

NIAGARA GREEN

December 29s just can't help them-selves—their incomparable zest for life just pours out of them. It would take a major disaster to stop the flow of your energy. What seems perfectly natural to you, however, others might find a bit over the top. Let them stand aside; your true friends won't mind getting soaked by your enthusiasm!

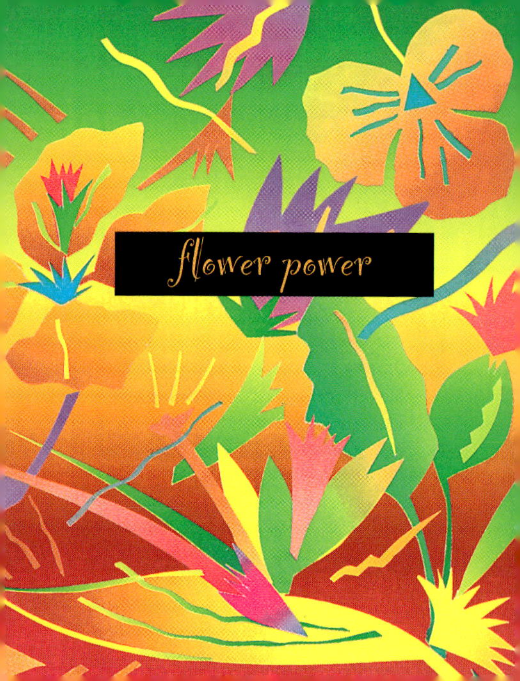
flower power

SNAPDRAGON

Godzilla you're not, but you *do* tend to have a dragon-sized temper. Although your outbursts can be practically scorching, you are forgiven almost immediately because you also have a dragon-sized heart. It's not easy being so volatile and vulnerable, but most December 29s have mastered the art of damage control. Your friends may sometimes be in awe of you, but they miss you when you're gone!

animal affinity

EAGLE

Sharp-eyed and alert, the eagle lazily glides along one moment and then swoops like a predator the next. In similar fashion, December 29s appear relaxed on the surface, but your "inner eye" is always tuned to the only prey that truly matters to you: the truth. Some call you a visionary, but all respect your unique ability to penetrate life's facades and expose the truth behind the shadows.

your first desire

LOVE

Desire for romance inspires most of the activities in your daily life, from riding the subway to having your teeth cleaned. You may have a patient heart, but you're also quite industrious and you'll search tirelessly for the grand payoff: true love!

your secret wish

December 29s tend to be critical of those who have too much, but they also have a few ideas about how to handle the excess of success! Yes, it's important to compose those poems, but wouldn't it be great if a Hollywood agent discovered your talent and contracted you to write a screenplay or two? Artistic integrity is fine, but it's even better on a full stomach!

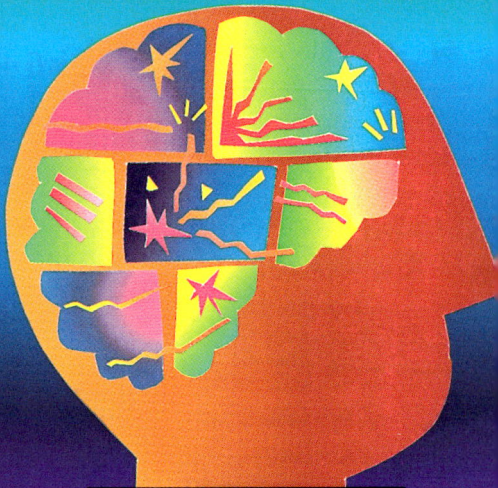

personality profile

What is "normal"? Most December 29s don't really know. Is it a nine-to-five job behind a big desk? Owning a sport-utility vehicle? Being a grandparent seven times over? Playing golf seven days a week?

Mold-breaker that you are, you cannot easily define your behavior and interests. One day you may be standing in line at the local Italian deli; the next week, you're a vegetarian! Did you enter college intending to study French, get a degree in psychology, and ultimately become an interior designer? Do you change your hairstyle every season? Welcome to the world of a December 29!

Your closest friends and relatives may not always understand what forces drive you—or what, exactly, you want out of life. But your gut does! December 29s tend to adhere to an "I'll know it when I see it" philosophy. This provides you with a wide-open mind as well as an unclouded desire for experience.

It is not uncommon for December 29s to change jobs, move to new cities, or develop different hobbies to keep their outlooks fresh. Because you trust your ability to achieve true greatness— whether personally, professionally, or creatively—you have learned that patience offers great rewards. Or if you don't know it yet, you soon will!

But December 29s work especially hard at achieving happiness. This is why, when all is said and done, companionship is so important to you. You seek symmetry in almost everything you do, so if you spend eight hours a day tallying up sales figures, then you should spend at least as much time in the proximity of a loved one (pets included)!

Many December 29s who are not in romantic relationships frequently become devoted to habitual forms of entertainment. Are you a die-hard Thursday night *Seinfeld* watcher? Do you awake early on Sunday mornings to do the crossword puzzle? Do you always treat yourself to a hot fudge sundae on Saturday afternoons?

December 29s are often admired for their childlike ability to seek pleasure from a variety of activities. Occasionally, however, they become discouraged by the sheer number of outlets for their ever-unfolding creativity. This is when you should remind yourself that you can travel across the rainbow by taking it one color at a time!

room for improvement

Y ou always have time for a friend. You always have time to take on more work. December 29s are extremely generous, and they always have time for everything—except maybe themselves. December 29s don't like to ask for help. Some don't really know how to ask for help. So sometimes you pretend you don't *need* help—even as your commitments threaten to overwhelm you!

A typical day in the life of a December 29 is often as full as an overstuffed couch! Try sitting down on a more comfortable, normal-size sofa once in a while—you deserve it!

Overdoing can lead to some serious mood swings. When your world is in order, you can savor even the most trifling pleasures in life, like a perfect cup of coffee or a favorite song on the radio. But when you're "stuck," you may go ballistic over the smallest of demands. December 29s often suffer silently, and continue to accommodate the needs of others instead of their own.

Maybe you secretly fear that what you've taken so long to build—honest, life-affirming connections with others—will deteriorate if you are not always strong. But even Superman cannot withstand the effects of kryptonite! Giving to others will do you very little good if you neglect yourself in the process.

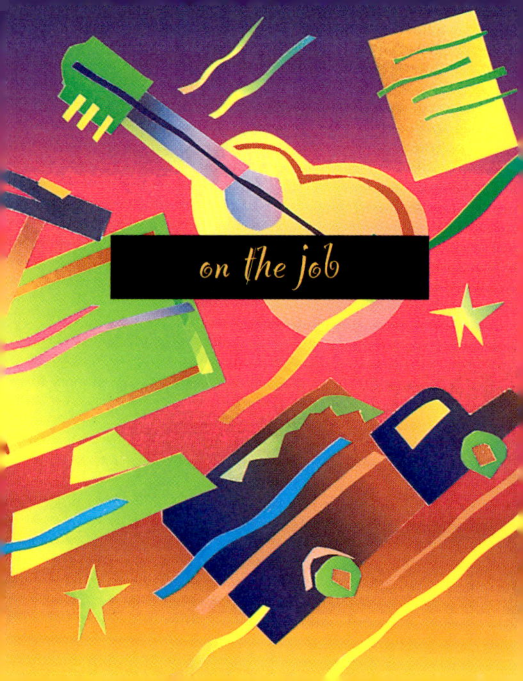
on the job

Is your ideal commute to work a stroll from the bedroom to the kitchen in your favorite slippers?

Most December 29s are well-equipped with "dream job" fantasies, and many would love to harmonize professional endeavors and personal desires. (Translation: A job that allows you to wear pajamas to the office!) Structure, however, is crucial to your life—even if you don't always know it!

On the job, December 29s generally obey an almost puritanical work ethic.

As a result, your colleagues tend to hold you in high esteem. But you cannot always return the compliments since you are easily agitated by the lack of creativity (or cooperation) among your associates . . . and superiors.

Because you are a born leader, you have a tendency to take control whenever and wherever possible. Sometimes this is the right thing to do—but sometimes it isn't. December 29s need to learn how to speak up and invite others to share the load. This would certainly make *your* life a lot easier!

December 29s always do a job well—but, at the end of the day, you know it's merely a means to an end. Whether it's a dream come true or a nightmare, a morass of overwork or a piece of cake, your job is a way station on the road to ultimate success. And that is the final dream!

at play

December 29s don't like to waste time—especially free time! You tend to be *very* serious about your leisurely pursuits, and you would prefer to stay clear of complicated planning.

A born dreamer, you are rarely at a loss for ways to entertain yourself, and there is no one formula for fun in your rule book. There aren't even five! A barbecue at the beach? Fine. But how about balancing your checkbook with crayons and highlighter pens, or color-coordinating your sock drawer? Now *that's* an activity for a December 29!

You tend to turn "musts" into "wants," and the word "boring" does not exist in your vocabulary. December 29s are masters at developing creative solutions for enduring the mundane chores of everyday life. In many ways, you are always at play!

But you also like to choose activities that offer a lot of reflective time; and if you're alone, you'd probably be more comfortable sitting under the shade of a sycamore tree than perching on a bar stool! December 29s are lucky: Pleasure is not hard for you to find. Choosing the right people to share it with, however, can prove to be your greatest challenge. But that's great, too, because the desire for romantic connection inspires most of your best pursuits, in any case!

home sweet home

Many December 29s find true re-laxation an exhausting task, so your comfort level at home is of the ut-most importance. Even if your private space is the size of a postage stamp, you're likely to treat it as a sanctuary of self-indulgence!

When it comes to physical surround-ings, most December 29s would rather have a house full of sentimental favorites than an abundance of fancy furniture. Your best friend's couch may be made of the finest leather, but your futon by the window is where you're most at ease.

As for home decorating, you're not likely to shop on Rodeo Drive—you're more apt to invent a chair out of a few pillows, a silk shawl, and a stack of milk crates! Need a night table? That's what a stack of books is for. This is not to say that December 29s do not have an appealing lifestyle. You do. It's just that your unique vision is your very own. And it generally wins its share of admirers.

You enjoy inviting guests over to your humble abode—but December

29s are also pretty finicky about who those guests are. In the privacy of your own home, you are only available to those with whom you truly want to share your time. (Many of whose pictures can probably be found framed upon the mantle!)

If you've ever stared at a ringing telephone and asked yourself, "Why bother?" then you are a true December 29! You like to be social on your *own* terms. Otherwise—why bother?

how do you love?

Y ou are a thoughtful and vocal lover, often dreaming of words to express the ever-expanding realm of your emotions.

Few December 29s adhere to "normal" rites of romantic passage. Neither designer cologne nor a bouquet of red roses can prove your love to another. You have a private way of communicating your feelings. Only your heart knows the language of which you speak.

But your capacity for love has its limits. Because most December 29s have experienced heartbreak before, they are apt to keep a watchful eye out for dishonesty or deception. You tend to be jealous; but you can also be easily turned off by possessiveness or too much overt affection. December 29s are acutely aware of the heart's many contradictions, and love, to them, can be a balancing act.

But your active mind can be put to rest by an even more active body. December 29s are famous as cultivated lovers who can turn the simplest activity into a moment of intense intimacy.

Like a conductor of a symphony orchestra, you can create beautiful music with the raising of a single finger.

December 29s may be gifted in the art of romantic expression, but they also require a wealth of understanding from their loved ones—no matter how much they pretend not to need attention. If you are still searching for that someone who speaks your language, have confidence and patience: Your dream lover is out there just waiting to hear your beautiful tunes!

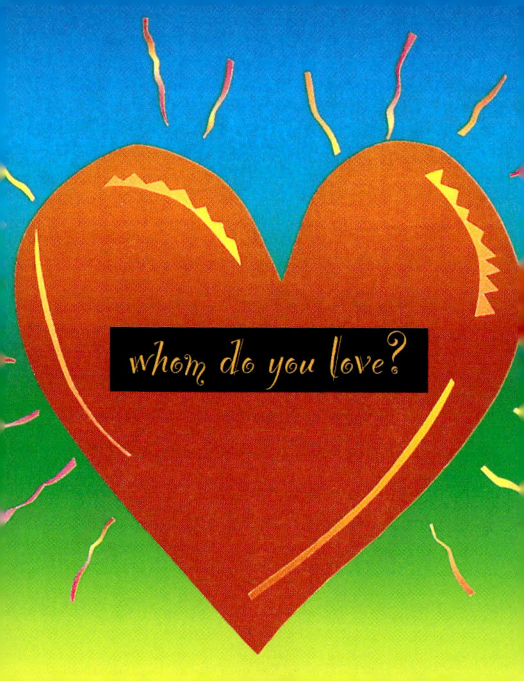
whom do you love?

D ecember 29s (Capricorn) get along best with:

Aries (March 21–April 20)
Taurus (April 21–May 21)
Virgo (August 24–September 23)
Scorpio (October 24–November 22)
Aquarius (January 21–February 19)
Pisces (February 20–March 20)

Ｄecember 29s (Capricorn) get along better without:

Gemini (May 22–June 21)
Cancer (June 22–July 23)
Leo (July 24–August 23)
Libra (September 24–October 23)
Sagittarius
   (November 23–December 21)
Capricorn
   (December 22–January 20)

December 29s seek out people who are:
stable, affectionate, self-disciplined, intellectual, loyal, and organized.

December 29s avoid people who are:
impulsive, argumentative, erratic, high-strung, financially careless, or pessimistic.

famous/infamous people born today

Nikolai Andrianov (1952) Olympic
  gymnast

Mary Tyler Moore (1937) actress, *The Dick
  Van Dyke Show*, *The Mary Tyler Moore Show*

Andrew Johnson (1808) seventeenth
  president of the United States;
  only president to be impeached

Tom Jarriel (1934) television journalist,
  20/20

Pablo Casals (1876) cellist

Kimberly Russell (1964) actress, *Head of the Class*

Jon Voight (1938) actor, *Midnight Cowboy, Coming Home*

Ray Thomas (1941) singer and flutist, Moody Blues, "Nights in White Satin"

Laffit Pincay Jr. (1946) jockey

Charles Goodyear (1800) inventor of "vulcanization" process for making rubber

Laurel Masse (1951) singer, the Manhattan Transfer, "Operator"

Ted Danson (1947) actor, *Cheers, Three Men and a Baby*

oh what a day it was

DECEMBER 29

First U.S. chapter of the YMCA is founded, in Boston (1851)

Boston resident Emma Snodgrass is arrested for wearing pants (1852)

Fred Newton swims the entire length of the Mississippi River (from Ford Dam, Minnesota, to New Orleans, Louisiana—a distance of 1,832 miles) in 742 hours (1930)

flashback: your past lives

In any past life, December 29s would have been in close connection to the earth—or its symbolic equivalent, the world of practicality. It is not unlikely that your past lives included the following occupations:

Mason
Gardener
Stone sculptor
Dynamiter
Grave digger
Lumberjack

your personal proverb

A road of a thousand miles begins with the first step.

English proverb

a word of advice

The one thing you can't control is time. December 29s may want to hit the fast-forward button and land immediately in the future, but what you need to understand is that a grand design is in order. Love may very well find you in the most unlikely of places. Remember, Cinderella obeyed her curfew and still got to wear a stunning pair of slippers!

looking ahead

What does every story have in common? Change. You can't get from the first chapter to the last without a plot. Character development can only occur when you are faced with adversity. Learn to appreciate your abilities—and shortcomings—when dealing with life's occasional struggles. Even heroes have their flaws!